THE
DARK CONTINENT

THE JOURNEY SERIES — BOOK 2

A LIFE OF DREAMS
JOHN McATEER

PUBLISHED BY FIDELI PUBLISHING, INC.

Copyright ©2021, John McAteer

ALL RIGHTS RESERVED.

No part of this publication may be reproduced, stored in a retrieval system, or transmitted in any form or by any means—electronic, mechanical, photo-copy, recording, or any other—except for brief quotation in reviews, without the prior permission of the author or publisher.

ISBN: 978-1-948638-18-0 (hardcover)

978-1-948638-18-0 (paperback)

Published by

Fideli Publishing, Inc.
119 W. Morgan St.
Martinsville, IN 46151

www.FideliPublishing.com

This book is dedicated to

John Bosco
Jerry Ippolito
Jerry Boren
Johnny Rodriquez
Michael Delfino
My family and friends

SPECIAL THANKS TO

Craig Boddington
Jim Bowman
Gus Congemi
Nancy Delfino
Mark Drury
Bob Foulkrod
Nancy Lee Gysin
Rob Keck
Garry Mason
Tom Nelson
Wayne Scott
Russ Thornberry
Brenda Valentine
Larry Weishuhn

Avula Safaris
Boone and Crockett Club
Buck Fever Scents
Legends of Outdoors
NWTF
Pope and Young Club
Safari Club International
Wild Sheep Foundation
& All the Dedicated Outfitters

John is one of my closest friends. He is someone, like myself, whose handshake is his contract. John has honed his hunting and fishing skills over his many years both in the field and mentoring others. I would highly recommend any of his books. A great heirloom for generations to come.

God bless John and may he enjoy many more adventures!

Bob Foulkrod

TABLE OF CONTENTS

Special Thanks v
   Testimonial from Bob Foulkrod vii

Introduction viii

The Hunt 1
   Testimonial from Larry Weishuhn 3

Zebra 9
   Testimonial from Gus Congemi 11

Wildebeest 21
   Craig Boddington 23

Gemsbok 31
   Testimonial from Rob Keck 33

Greater Kudu 43
   Testimonial from Mark Drury 45

Duiker 53
   Testimonial from Brenda Valentine 55

Blesbok 61
   Testimonial from Garry Mason 63

Impala 71
   Testimonial from Tom Nelson 73

Warthog 81
   Testimonial from Russ Thornberry 83

Steenbok **91**
   Testimonial from Nancy Lee Gysin.................................94

Red Lechwe..**101**
   Testimonial from Jim Bowman.......................................103

Something to Chew On...**113**

Friends and Fellow Hunters..**117**

Closing Statement..**125**

AFRICA

SOUTH AFRICA

INTRODUCTION

Caught Between Two Different Worlds

Hunting has been a passion of mine since I was a young man. Learning the skills to overcome what Mother Nature can throw at you is always a challenge. I found myself caught between what seemed like two different worlds, North America and Africa, I had just spent most of my hunting career in the vast wilderness of North America, Canada, and the Arctic, then moved south to Mexico and on to Tibet chasing my dreams and testing myself and my ability to learn and overcome any obstacles in my path. I faced some pretty hard feats of endurance as I attacked mountains and waterways while dealing with uncooperative weather conditions.

I always tried to escape everyday living and chase the shadows of the unknown in different parts of the world. With every adventure's beginning and subsequent end, I felt myself aging, and aches and pains were starting to creep into my life more and more often. Trying to stay fit was now a chore, and training for a hunt, while crucial and enjoyable, became more difficult each year. As they say, time stands still for no one.

When I sit in my trophy room, I find myself inundated by memories of my past hunts, both the successful ones and the ones that didn't end as well as I'd hoped. I realize I was truly blessed to be able to live out all of my dreams and continue seeking out adventure and new conquests at every turn. Never one to stand still for long, I decided I was going to look at Africa for my next quest.

PREPARING FOR THE TRIP

At this point, Africa was a bit of an unknown entity to me. I only knew what I had read in journals and books when I was younger and what I'd soaked up about the great hunters and their experiences as they entered the Dark Continent for the first time.

After reading more about Africa, I realized there were many dangers an individual might have to face while hunting its vast wilderness. These were things I'd never had to consider when hunting anywhere else. So, I adopted the attitude of expecting the worst and hoping for the best.

I started studying different countries located in Africa and the types of game available in each. I also made sure I understood weather conditions for the time of year I planned to be there. Even with all my studying, I was in

The Dark Continent

Meeting of David Livingstone (1813-1873) and Henry Morton Stanley (1841-1904), Africa, ca. 1875-ca. 1940, International Mission Photography Archive, ca.1860-ca.1960.

Here's a little history lesson for you. Henry Morton Stanley was probably the first to use the phrase Dark Continent in his 1878 travelogue, Through the Dark Continent. The name stuck, probably because of the mysteries and the savagery people expected to find in Africa's interior.

Henry Morton Stanley, the adopted name of John Rowlands from North Wales, became famous for saying, "Dr. Livingstone, I presume," after finding Dr. David Livingstone, the famous explorer of Africa, near Lake Tanganyika in present-day Tanzania.

uncharted waters, but felt confident I could take on this journey and make it a success.

After studying, I reached out to several outfitters before making the decision of who I'd go with. A top-notch professional hunter named Gearhart Geyer of Yanni Safaris was the individual I felt fit my needs best.

The African topography was so different from I was used to when hunting in North America and Canada. South Africa and the area I had selected for the hunt was mostly prairie with slight rolling hills. My lifelong friend John Bosco, a frequent hunting companion on my many adventures, would be joining me on this trip.

THE TRIP IS ON

So, with that decided, I called my travel agent and asked her to arrange for us to travel from New York to Johannesburg during the month of August. Unlike New York, where June through August is summer, this time of year in Africa is considered winter. The average temperature during our trip would only reach about 64° (18°C), with the average low being a cool 46°F (8°C). I was confident this hunt would be extremely comfortable, and was looking forward to the cooler temperatures.

The length of travel time for this trip would present a new challenge for me, since the average flight time New York to Johannesburg was about 20 hours. I knew if I wanted to arrive fresh and rested, I would have to find a way to sleep during the long flight. This was easier said than done. I was way too excited about going to Africa and knew I wouldn't be able to stop thinking about it during the flight.

We would be landing in Johannesburg, the largest city in South Africa and the capital of the Gauteng province. This area, settled in 1886, has an interesting history of gold-mining and is the original home of Nelson Mandela.

My excitement grew to a new fever pitch as the jumbo jet touched down at Tambo International Airport. We were finally at our destination!

Gathering my gear after leaving the plane, I realized that I'd packed a lot more than usual for this trip. I guess I was worried about being so far from home and not having all the equipment I might need.

As John went through customs, I was busy looking for my professional hunter (PH) and daydreaming about what I would encounter on this trip. Stories and legends about Africa kept my mind busy. I was excited to be here, even though Johannesburg has a reputation of being one of the most dangerous cities in the world. To balance that ugliness, it's also home to some of the most beautiful national parks, including Kruger Park and the Limpopo River Valley. These parks have been set aside for preservation and animal conservation.

I finally spotted our PH, Gearhart Geyer. After greeting us, he suggested we spend the night at his home in Johannesburg so we could get a fresh start the next morning. We arrived at his home and settled in for a relaxing evening with his wife and children. We were treated to a beautiful traditional African dinner along with some superb red wine.

HEADING TO CAMP

Morning came early, but the smell of fresh brewed coffee lured me out of bed and after having a cup, the day officially started to take shape. After breakfast, we loaded our gear into a safari truck and started on the five-hour drive to our hunting destination. During the trip our PH told us about the area where we would be hunting. Our destination was a concession area that bordered Kruger National Park.

The drive was amazing, and five hours went by quickly. I was amazed by how many vineyards we passed. It was almost like being in California wine country. When we arrived, we were greeted by a beautiful hunting camp consisting of a main building, five outbuildings and a large fire pit area. The fire pit, or story pit as I like to think of it, looked like the perfect place to gather and tell hunting stories and brag about our wild adventures.

We unloaded our gear at our respected cabins, or rondavels as their known in South Africa. A rondavel is a round hut with a thatched roof. It's simple and easily made from local easily found materials. The walls are mud, the roof is grass, and the floor is packed cow dung. Inside each were three beds with mosquito netting and a full-sized bathroom. The furnishings were simple local artifacts, giving the décor a true African theme.

South Africa is the most popular hunting destination for die-hard hunters. The variety of game found here is amazing, and far more than I was expecting. Besides boasting one of the best areas to harvest the big five, there are also Cape buffalo, elephant rhino, lions, and myriad plains game are all found in this region.

Cape Buffalo

COMMENTS ABOUT JOHN FROM LARRY WEISHUHN...

"John McAteer is at it again, and I'm telling you it's in a good way, this time with a book about some of his African hunting adventures. Having been to Africa a few times, I can tell you there is something about that continent that attaches itself to you heart and mind and creates a near unquenchable 'thirst' the first time you step out in 'the bush' to return again and again. It's a thirst that can only be satiated, albeit momentarily, by returning to experience the thorn bush to pit your skills against the horned, clawed and big-teethed animals which live there. John, with his stories found in this tome will help you recall all your adventures if you have been there, and, if Africa is still on your list, will make you want to make the journey there ever more wanting!"

Sincerely,

Larry Weishuhn

John Bosco and a California client.

DAY ONE

It was cool morning that very first day and a light jacket was my first choice as we sat down and had a great breakfast consisting of a variety of game meats, ostrich eggs, fruit, coffee and fresh squeezed juice I knew I wasn't in Kansas anymore.

Before we headed out on our very first day my PH discussed camp policy and what was expected of each hunter when we were afield. After this brief meeting, it was time to begin our adventure. We proceeded to gather our equipment and our rifles for a long day on Safari. My quest was a

Cape Buffalo, also known to most African hunters as black death. As the name indicates, they are unpredictable and quite dangerous. I was also looking to do some great plains game hunting.

We rode in the special safari trucks that perch the hunter above the truck in elevated seats, giving the hunter a better field-of-view. We left camp at 6:30 a.m. and proceeded to view some of what the Dark Continent had to offer.

Another history lesson: Joseph Thomson, a 25-year-old Scotsman, and a small group of men left Mombasa on March 15, 1883; their destination was the shore of Lake Victoria. They were only the second group of explorers to tread on Maasai territory. During his trip, Thomson discovered and named several Kenyan landmarks, including the Aberdare Range, and Thomson Falls, which he dedicated to his father. His name lingers today in the Thompson's gazelle, one of the most recognizable inhabitants of the African Savannah.

I was amazed by the amount of game we were seeing as we made our journey, and it wasn't long before our tracker saw some fresh buffalo tracks. I was excited, to say the least. I jumped from the truck and proceeded to grab my 375 H&H and chambered a 300-grain bullet into the barrel and finished loading my rifle.

We followed the buffalo's tracks for about three hours. We finally came across 10 buffalo. We paid attention to the direction of the wind as we approached the buffalo. We decided to be cautious as we closed our approach. Never having seen a Cape buffalo in my life, I was amazed by the enormous size of the beast. I was awed by the tremendous strength they exhibited as we watched them trekking back and forth through the thickets.

I closed the gap to 100 yards, and then down to 50. At this point, I started glassing each Buffalo. I was checking out the size of the horns to see if they would meet the criteria I was looking for. The wind was in my favor and I had plenty of time to study these great animals. It was incredible.

A fully mature buffalo has been known to hold off a pride of lions, and can even kill them by impaling them on their massive horns. After studying the bulls, I decided that none of them were what I was looking for.

It was a long and somewhat disappointing day, but even so I was still having the time of my life. As a season hunter, I have learned patience and don't take down just any quarry. I have developed my focus and only kill what I am looking for. I would rather go home empty handed than harvest an immature animal. Doing this lets the younger animals grow into something magnificent.

So, my first day on Safari was on the books and I had another deposit in my memory bank.

COMMENTS ABOUT JOHN FROM GUS CONGEMI...

John has not disappointed. His first book was a great read and this one is even better. John is an exceptional outdoorsman, hunter and storyteller. His passion for what he does is evident, and he has a unique way of translating it to his readers. You will feel like you are there with him.

Congratulations and continued success, John!

Gus Congemi
Live the Wild Life
Square Vision Productions

DAY TWO

Our second day was upon me so quickly, I was hardly prepared for the morning light that hit me when I opened my eyes. After downing some caffeine, my excitement was back and I was wide awake and ready for a new adventure. I had decided we'd continue looking for my majestic Cape Buffalo.

We headed to the same area where we saw the buffalo the previous day, and stumbled upon a herd of Burchell's zebras. We got out of the truck and quickly decided to delay our quest for buffalo, choosing to put a plan together to get in front of the traveling zebra herd instead. Ultimately, we wanted them to pass in front of our position.

It took us approximately two hours to maneuver into a good position. It was a waiting game now. Time was on our side, and the wait was worth it. There were about eight zebras, one of which was a really beautiful stallion. He was a tough guy, and carried some battle scars from fighting with other males.

I made my choice and took out my Winchester 375 H&H safari rifle. I got settled and homed in on the zebra's shoulder area. I took a deep breath and squeezed the trigger. My 300-grain bullet found its mark, and I had a beautiful Burchell's zebra. My first African animal was in the books.

I always believe in paying my respects to the animals I have just harvested. One way to do this is to take a nice picture, so that's what we did. I could not have been happier with this animal.

As we were loading my beautiful zebra into the truck (thank God for an electric winch), I gazed to my right and saw a small herd of Impalas and springbok. It was a beautiful sight. The topography of the land was so flat that you could see for miles. The plains reminded me of hunting antelope in Wyoming.

At about 1 p.m., we decided to have a great infield lunch with all the trimmings. It was a good time to relax and talk about the hunt and the great zebra I had just taken.

During lunch, we decided to look for the Gemsbok we'd seen earlier in the day. One good thing about hunting in Africa is, even though my main quarry was a Cape Buffalo it was easy to hunt a variety of other game along the way. There were so many different species of game that during the course of the day there were lots of choices.

As the sun set behind the beautiful African acacia trees, we put a close to our second day. When we arrived at camp, we drew on our last bit of energy to sit around the campfire telling stories after our great meal.

I really enjoyed listening to everybody's stories about what they had seen during the course of the first two days, as well as some of the great stories that our PH told us about previous hunts. He had some dangerous encounters with some of his clients, and said that made his job more enjoyable.

My friend Joseph Ferraro also harvested a zebra.

BRAISED ZEBRA

INGREDIENTS

Two pounds of zebra, cut into chunks.

One pound tomatoes, peeled seeded and chopped.

Two onions, chopped

Two TBS flour

One Tsp. paprika.

Pinches salt, pepper, turmeric, coriander, cayenne.

One cup browned bone stock.

Quarter cup olive oil.

Quarter cup heavy cream.

A good jigger of sherry.

INSTRUCTIONS

Fry the onion golden in the oil and remove to a plate.

Dust the meat with flour, salt, and pepper, and brown in oil.

Add tomatoes and onions to the pan, stir briefly to take up the crusty bits on the bottom of the pan, then add the sherry, stock, and spices.

Simmer until tender, which may take a while if the beast was old. Before serving, whisk in the heavy cream.

MABOKAY

INGREDIENTS

Two pounds of zebra, cut into chunks

Two cups of crumbled roasted peanuts

Juice from one or two lemons

Two large onions, chopped

Half a dozen chopped green chilies

Plantain leaf – one or two whole leaves

INSTRUCTIONS

Cook the peanuts, meat, and onion with a little water for about twenty minutes. It should be a stiff glop.

Take a leaf and pull off the central rib (cut across the rib, flip the edge of the blade underneath the rib, and pull). Trim the leaf to a large rectangle. Sprinkle some salt on the leaf, and place the meat mixture on one side. Flavor it with the lemon juice and chilies.

Now fold over all ends to make a secure package within several layers of plantain leaf, and tie it up like a postage parcel. Place on a rack in a large pot and steam for over an hour.

Unwrap at the table and serve with corn mush.

The Dark Continent

ZEBRA STAMPOT

INGREDIENTS

Two pounds of zebra, cut into chunks

Two onions, chopped

Two tomatoes, peeled, seeded, and chopped

Two green plantain, peeled and chunked

Two sweet potatoes, chunked

Two or three chilies, minced

Two large regular potatoes, chunked

One can (one and half cup) coconut milk (santen)

One or two cups browned bone stock

Minced garlic, ginger

Salt, pepper, plus pinches of ground clove and nutmeg

INSTRUCTIONS

Rub the garlic, ginger, chilies, salt, and pepper into the meat, and let it rest for one or two hours in the refrigerator.

Then brown it in a heavy casserole with a little oil. When it is well seared, add the stock and spices and simmer for an hour.

Then add the vegetables and scant water to cover. Simmer until the vegetables are tender.

When vegetables are cooked, mash them with a potato masher. If using meat on the bone from an odd cut, it would be a good idea to remove it from the bones before mashing.

Mix in the coconut milk before serving.

WILDEBEEST

COMMENTS ABOUT JOHN FROM CRAIG BODDINGTON...

It's not unusual for Africa to get in your blood! I went for the first time thinking I could get it out of my system once and for all...and that didn't work very well! Another thing about Africa is that many of us feel compelled to tell our stories. That's a good thing, and we're fortunate that my friend John McAteer suffers from both complaints: Like most of us who have been there, he can't get Africa out of his system... and he's driven to share his experience! John McAteer has hunted widely throughout much of the world...he has great stories and tells them well! I look forward to reading the rest of his African adventures...at least for now!

Craig Boddington

DAY THREE

Day three started in an unusual way. First thing, we received a phone call from the local game constable who alerted to a blue wildebeest siting. The wildebeest was attacked by a pack of African wild dogs between Kruger National forest on one side and our concession area on the other, He said it appeared the wildebeest had been attacked by a pack of wild African dogs and was injured.

The constable wanted to know if my PH had a hunter in camp that would like to go out and dispatch this injured animal. Of course, I volunteered. So, we headed to the firebreak.

This area was fenced off to create a firebreak between the park and private concession area. It was approximately 80 yards wide and about 500 yards long. My PH told me that the blue wildebeest is the poor man's buffalo, and when injured it has the ability to charge, and most likely will. He wanted my assurance that I would not run if this happened. I assured him that I would stand my ground.

We didn't see the animal as we entered the area, so we positioned ourselves parallel to each other at about 40 yards apart. We slowly walked the 500-yard distance. Suddenly, here came the charging wounded wildebeest straight at me! I held my ground and let him close the distance to about 60 yards. My PH decided to take a shot then, but missed. Once this happened, the wildebeest turned and went straight for my PH!

Before he could chamber a new round, I turned and fired my round when the animal was only 20 yards from my professional hunter, I hit the mark, and the animal fell 10 feet in front of the professional hunter also known as a PH. He thanked me for my shot and said I could hunt with him anytime, anywhere. I had proven myself a good hunter.

I had been frozen like a rock as I took my shot, and didn't realize I was standing in a thorn bush. Once the adrenaline wore off, I realized my legs were cut up pretty badly.

We examined the wildebeest and saw that its lips were torn, its tail bitten and half eaten, and its back straps on its legs pretty badly shredded. The animal was in pretty bad shape.

This adventure was a rush. Needless to say, my PH whipped up one heck of a story when we hit the fire pit that night.

WILDEBEEST SIRLOIN

INGREDIENTS FOR SIRLOIN

- 1/2 tsp salt
- 1 lb. wildebeest sirloin, sinew removed
- 2 cups good-quality dry red wine
- 1 Tbs black peppercorns
- 2 Tbs chopped fresh root ginger
- 2 Tbs cinnamon sticks
- 1/2 tsp grated nutmeg
- 1 pinch saffron
- 2 Tbsp. brown sugar
- 1 cup water
- 1 Tbsp. butter
- 1 Tbsp. sunflower oil

INSTRUCTIONS

Rub the salt into the meat and refrigerate for 1 hour.

Place the remaining ingredients in a saucepan and bring to boil. Leave to cool.

Once cool, pour the marinade over the meat and refrigerate overnight.

The following day, remove the meat and pat dry.

Reserve the marinade.

Preheat the oven to 425°F (220° C).

Heat one Tbsp. (15 ml) olive oil in a frying pan and add 1 tsp (5 ml) butter. Add the meat and brown well.

Place the meat in the oven and cook to desired doneness; 3-4 minutes for medium-rare.

LEG OF BEEST

YOGURT MARINADE

This recipe is for a leg of wildebeest larger than large a leg of lamb)

Marinate meat overnight in a plastic bag using enough plain yogurt to cover.

Next day, rinse the yogurt off, dry the piece of meat and rub it well with the following mixture:

RUB INGREDIENTS

- 1/2 cup flour
- 2 heaped tablespoons of your favorite barbecue spice (or make your own — see below)
- 1 heaped tablespoon of salt
- 1/2 tablespoon of fine pepper
- 1 tablespoon of paprika

INSTRUCTIONS

In a deep roasting pan add about 7 cloves of garlic.

Add water mixed with a little vinegar to roasting pan, keep adding this mix throughout roasting.

Roast in slow oven at 330°F (170°C)

Roast time will be according to size, for large leg: about around 2 hours or more.

BARBECUE SPICE MIX

- 1/2 cup brown sugar
- 1/2 cup paprika
- 1 tablespoon ground black pepper
- 1 tablespoon salt
- 1 tablespoon chili powder
- 1 tablespoon garlic powder
- 1 tablespoon onion powder

GEMSBOK

COMMENTS ABOUT JOHN FROM ROB KECK...

This legendary hunter provides a mix of African Adventure, danger and how to from his vast experiences of hunting the Dark Continent. In many ways he's like your best hunting buddy taking you along on the Journey. John's easy style makes this an enjoyable read and helps one understand why he is known as "The Educator" as well as "The Legend Behind the Scenes".

Rob Keck

DAY FOUR

This turned out to be another hard day looking for my Cape Buffalo. As hard as we all tried, I still had no luck. I must've looked at more than 20 Buffalo that morning and still couldn't find one mature enough for my purposes.

We saw a promising herd of Cape Buffalo and tried to close the distance. The buffalo caught site of us and was alerted to our presence, and just as quickly as we'd seen them, they disappeared. Discouraged, we headed back to our vehicles.

On the way back, we saw some gemsbok in the far distance. As you know, a gemsbok is a large analog genus Oryx. It is native to the arid regions of South Africa and also the Kalahari Desert. Males can reach a live weight of about 600 pounds and they can survive severe temperatures at both ends of the scale.

They tend to rest in the shade, due to a specific physiological adaptation that helps them cope with extreme temperatures. Like a dog, they cool off by panting. They are usually adapted to feeding at night, as plants will expose their growth more in the evening and hold a lot more moisture during the cooler nights.

Since we'd spotted them, we decided to go after the small herd for a few hours. We hoped this would increase our odds of harvesting a respectable specimen. We tried to get close, we got winded on the second attempt. The third time was my lucky charm. I took my Browning 7 mm and managed to work my way to within 100 yards of my prey. With one well-placed shot, I had just taken my second great trophy. Boy, was I proud of it!

The Dark Continent

My friend Joseph Ferraro and a gemsbok he harvested.

GEMSBOK FILLET

INGREDIENTS

1 gemsbok fillet, 1/2 lb.
olive oil
3 Tbsp. butter
1/2 onion, thinly sliced
1 clove garlic, crushed
1 cup mixed mushrooms such as shiitake, Portobello, bellini, etc.
1 cup shredded cabbage
1 cup good beef stock
1/2 cup (100ml) cream;
1 cup port
sprigs of rosemary
olive oil
salt and freshly ground pepper

INSTRUCTIONS

Clean the fillet and cut it into two portions

To make the fricassee, heat a little olive oil and a tablespoon of butter in a pan. Add the onion and slowly cook until it's slightly caramelized.

Turn up the heat and add the garlic and the mushrooms, along with another tablespoon of butter. Cook on high heat until the mushrooms are just tender, then add the cabbage and stir-fry for 1 minute.

Finish with a tablespoon of beef stock and the cream. Leave to simmer until the cream has reduced. Season to taste.

Next, heat a heavy frying pan to smoking. Add a dash of olive oil and a tablespoon of butter. Sear the meat well, then lower the heat and leave to cook to desired doneness. Remove from pan and let rest. Deglaze the pan with port, add the stock and a sprig of rosemary and let it reduce until thickened.

To serve, spoon the fricassee into the middle of the plate, top with the sliced gemsbok and pour the port jus over the top.

GEMSBOK STIR-FRY

MARINADE INGREDIENTS

2 Tbsp. Shaoxing wine or dry sherry

1/2 tsp salt

3 Tbsp. soy sauce

1 Tbsp. potato or corn starch mixed with 2 tablespoons water

STIR-FRY INGREDIENTS

1 lb. gemsbok, trimmed of fat

1-1/2 cups peanut or other cooking oil

1 to 4 fresh red chilies

3 garlic cloves, slivered

1 Tbsp. soy sauce

1 red or yellow bell pepper, sliced

1 bunch cilantro, roughly chopped

2 tsp sesame oil

rice, enough for each serving of stir-fry

INSTRUCTIONS

Stir marinade ingredients together in large bowl or add to plastic bag large enough to hold meat.

Slice the meat into thin slivers — 1-3 inches long and about 1/4 inch wide. Mix with the marinade and set aside while you cut all the other ingredients and prepare rice for cooker or stove-top cooking. Time this so that it will be finished cooking by the time your stir-fry is ready.

Heat the peanut oil in a wok or large heavy pot until it reaches 275°F to 290°F. Don't let it get too hot. Add about 1/3 of the meat to the hot oil and use a chopstick or butter knife to separate the meat slices the second they hit the hot oil. Let them sizzle for 30 seconds to 1 minute. Remove with a spider skimmer or slotted spoon. Set aside and cook the remaining meat one-third at a time.

Pour out all but about 3 tablespoons of the oil.

Place the pan with the remaining hot oil over high heat. The moment it begins to smoke, add the chilies and bell peppers and stir-fry for 90 seconds. Next, add the garlic and cook another 30 seconds, then add the cooked meat and stir fry another 90 seconds.

Add the cilantro and soy sauce, then stir fry a final 30 seconds, or just until the cilantro wilts. Turn off the heat and stir in the sesame oil.

Serve at once with steamed rice.

GREATER KUDU

COMMENTS ABOUT JOHN FROM MARK DRURY...

To all my hunting brothers and Sisters, John McAteer has once again brought his adventures to pen and paper and is sharing them with all of us.

If you have been to Africa this book will help bring back special memories of the Dark Continent. If however, you are like me and have never been there, John's writings will inspire you to go!

Congratulations on another fine work of art John. Thank you for sharing your heart and soul with all of us. Thank you for bringing the Dark Continent into our homes, cabins and blinds!

Mark Drury
Drury Outdoors

DAY FIVE

We approached our fifth day, I was not concentrating on buffalo this time. We'd decided we were going to go after kudu today. One of the problems we faced in this next challenge was the kudu's habitat. The vast plains allowed the kudu to spot us from long distances. We would have to be cautious on this stalk.

I was after the greater kudu this time. This animal is common in South Africa. They can reach a weight of 600 pounds, can attain a length of 72 inches, and have been clocked 40 mph in a dead run. They like arid conditions but are also found in the hill country. Their main predation, like most animals in South Africa, comes from lions, leopards, spotted hyenas and believe it or not the African python. These huge snakes have been known to take down newborn kudu.

We spent a good part of the morning watching for kudu. Eventually we decided to address our growling stomachs. We'd skipped breakfast that morning, so lunch was sounding pretty good right about then.

As soon as I took my lunch out, I caught movement out of the corner of my eye. It was far away, so I picked up my binoculars to take a closer look. There were three bull kudu standing right there. My hunger was forgotten as we started laying out a game plan.

The three were in a large open area about 500 yards from us. We studied every option, and could only come up with one answer. A five-foot anthill was the only thing available to be our cover — everything else was grass. Let the challenge begin!

We estimated if we took our time, it would take us about two hours of deliberate movement to reach the anthill. As I prepared to make this trek, I figured I'd be shooting from about a 300-yard distance. I was used to taking long shots because of all of the mountain sheep hunts I'd been on, so I felt comfortable with this shot.

The Dark Continent

Eventually, after all that slow movement, I was in a good spot. I was covered by the anthill, so when the time came I was totally locked on my target. At a range of 347 yards, the kudu was in my sites. I was using my 7 MM with 150-grain bullets.

I took the shot, and put it right into the boiler room. My kudu went about 80 yards and folded. He was an absolutely beautiful bull with horns reaching 49 to 50 inches with nice ivory tips. Now the work began, loading him up and getting him back to camp.

As we headed back to camp, we came across what I considered the greatest African trophy animal around — the white rhino. To me this is one of the big five.

They are known as even-toed ungulates in the rhino family. The white rhino can tip the scales at 5,000 pounds and can reach a top speed of 31 mph. This animal's biggest predation comes in the form of poaching. Rhino poaching has escalated over the years due to the demand from Asian markets. Their entire range of habitat is threatened.

I believe there are only 5,000 of these animals left in the wild in Africa. The rhino horns are used in ornamental carvings and for traditional medicine. They say it can cure hangovers, cancer and impotency.

Seeing this beautiful specimen running free with its small calf truly made my trip complete.

MARINATED GRILLED KUDU

INGREDIENTS

Kudu loin cut into 2-inch pieces
1/2 cup coriander leaves
1/2 cup sweet basil
1/3 cup lemon juice
1/2 cup Italian flat leaf parsley
1/2 cup olive oil
2 Tbsp. dark soy sauce
5 cloves garlic, crushed

INSTRUCTIONS

Mix all ingredients together in plastic bag, then add meat and let it marinate overnight in fridge.

Grill over very hot coals for 2.5 minutes on each side for medium rare meat.

KALAHARI SALTED KUDU WITH SWEET POTATOES

INGREDIENTS

- 2-3 Tbsp. coarse sea salt
- 1 Tbsp. freshly crushed garlic
- 3 Tbsp. fresh chopped herbs (rosemary, thyme, oregano)
- 2 Tbsp. freshly ground black pepper
- 1/2 Tbsp. (10 ml) olive oil
- 1 whole kudu fillet approximately 4 lbs.
- 1 lb sweet potatoes, scrubbed, left unpeeled, and cut into thin slices
- 2 Tbsp. olive oil
- Sea Salt for sprinkling on potatoes

INSTRUCTIONS FOR KUDU

Mix the Sea Salt (coarse), crushed garlic, fresh herbs, black pepper and olive oil.

Roll the fillet in this mixture, rubbing it onto the meat so that it sticks.

Braise over hot to medium coals. Turn the fillet until it is cooked to your liking. If oven roasting, sear the fillet first by browning on each side in a large frying pan. Finish off in a hot oven at 400°F for about 20-35 minutes depending on how well done you would like it.

Rest for a few minutes before slicing into thick medallions. Season to taste.

INSTRUCTIONS FOR SWEET POTATOES

Arrange sweet potato slices in a baking dish. Drizzle with olive oil and roast them at 350°F for about 30 minutes, or until they are golden and crisp. Sprinkle with coarse sea salt and serve with the fillet.

DUIKER

COMMENTS ABOUT JOHN FROM BRENDA VALENTINE...

"Once you have experienced Africa, you can never fully leave Africa and Africa will never completely leave you. The land, the people, the animals, the rhythm of life on the dark continent is unlike anywhere I've ever been. My memories of Africa are among my greatest treasures.

Thank you John for sharing yours."

Brenda Valentine

DAY SIX

Monday, day six, we decided to change plans and scenery and head to a new area. This new location was a bit more rugged and I was excited to see what we would find.

The difference in terrain was refreshing. There was more vegetation growing along the hills, and there were trees up on a tiny ridge overlooking a small valley. There was a little waterhole there, so we decided to do some glassing.

My PH noticed a common Duiker, so we said decided to give him a chase. The common Duiker is also known as the gray or bush Duiker. It is a small antelope found in both South Africa and the Sahara. There are about 22 different species of antelope.

When in danger, these animals have a habit of running in a zigzag pattern. This type of running helps them to escape danger. They are tiny and have only a 10-year lifespan. There is very little known about this animal's behavior outside of its escape maneuvers.

This was another adventure for me, and I was sure it was going to turn out to be one of the easiest stalks of the trip. We managed to get within 85 yards and at that point I closed the deal with my 7mm. Suddenly, I had another beautiful specimen.

The Dark Continent

DUIKER GOULASH

INGREDIENTS

1 pound ground Duiker
1/4 cup chopped green bell pepper
1/4 cup chopped onion
2 tablespoons chopped fresh chives
15 1/4 ounces whole kernel corn, drained
2 red potatoes (cubed)
1 stalk celery (thinly sliced)
1 tomato (chopped)
42 ounces beef broth
1 cup water
1 cup elbow macaroni
salt
black pepper
1/4 teaspoon garlic powder (or to taste)

INSTRUCTIONS

Stir the Duiker, bell pepper, onion, and chives together in a large pot over medium heat until the vegetables are very tender and the Duiker has browned, about 10 minutes.

Stir in the corn, red potatoes, celery, tomato, beef broth, water, and macaroni. Bring to a boil over high heat; reduce heat to medium-low, cover, and simmer until the potatoes are tender — about 30 minutes more.

Season to taste with salt, pepper, and garlic powder before serving.

GRILLED BACON-WRAPPED DUIKER TENDERLOIN

INGREDIENTS
1 Duiker loin
8 oz. bacon
3/4 cup dry red wine
1/4 cup soy sauce
2 tsp dry mustard
1 Tbsp. honey
steak seasoning (see recipe below)
1 Tbsp. fresh thyme
1 Tbsp. fresh rosemary
2 tsp. Worcestershire sauce
1 Tbsp. brown sugar

STEAK SEASONING
2 Tbsp. crushed black pepper
2 Tbsp. garlic powder
2 Tbsp. kosher salt
2 Tbsp. paprika
1 Tbsp. onion powder
1 Tbsp. ground coriander
1 Tbsp. dried dill
1 Tbsp. crushed red pepper flakes

INSTRUCTIONS

In a glass measuring cup mix the wine, soy sauce, dry mustard powder, Worcestershire sauce, honey and brown sugar. Using butcher's twine, tie the loin in a log shape. Place the loin in a heavy-duty zip-lock bag and pour marinade in. Place on a dish and set in refrigerator for 1-2 hours.

Prepare charcoal grill for indirect heat. Light the grill and wait until it reaches medium heat (350° F).

Remove loin from marinade, blot with paper towels, remove the butcher's twine. Sprinkle liberally with the steak seasoning, fresh thyme and rosemary. Wrap meat with bacon.

Cook over medium heat until the internal temperature reaches 135° F. Cover and rest 15 minutes before slicing.

BLESBOK

COMMENTS ABOUT JOHN FROM GARRY MASON...

John McAteer has traveled and hunted the plains of Africa many times during his career as a legendary outdoorsman. His exploits and adventures on the Dark Continent are brought back to reality in this brand-new book. Sit back as we travel with John throughout the plains and savannas of Africa while chasing some of the most sought-after game species in the world of big game hunting. I know that you will enjoy each hair-raising adventure as we share the memories of these great hunts by my friend and Legends of the Outdoors Hall of Fame member, John McAteer. Few men travel where many dream of going.

Garry Mason
Founder/CEO Legends of the Outdoors Hall of Fame

DAY SEVEN

This day was dedicated to looking for a nice Blesbok (*Damaliscus pygargus phillipsi*). This animal, a member of the antelope family, is found in South Africa and Swaziland. It has a distinctive white face and forehead, which inspired its name — *bles* is the Afrikaans word for blaze, similar to the blaze found on a horse's forehead. It is truly a majestic looking antelope.

Our tracker had seen a small herd feeding in the tall grass about 10 miles due north from our camp the previous day. He'd also seen a few cheetahs not to far from them.

We fueled the truck and loaded enough gear for a long day. My PH said that if the cats where following the Blesbok, they might be covering a lot of clay during the day. (Clay referring to the red ground found in this area.)

The Ph was right about them covering a lot of real estate. We finally found the herd about 8 miles from where they were the day before. The long trip was worth it when we sited about 20 Blesbok.

This was going to be an easy stalk because we had good cover and there were about seven three-foot tall ant hills that were staggered across the plains in front of us. As we maneuvered into position, I struggled to find a good rest for the shot.

Ultimately, I decided to take an off-shoulder shot and use my 7mm mag. I took a 200-yard shot and was able to harvest a beautiful Blonde Blesbok.

The Dark Continent

BLESBOK CURRY

INGREDIENTS

2 1/2 inch fresh ginger, peeled and chopped

5 garlic cloves, peeled and chopped

2-3 fresh green chilies, chopped

1 Tbsp. whole coriander seeds

1/4 cup olive oil

2 medium onions, thinly sliced

1/4 tsp ground turmeric

2 lbs. Blesbok backstrap, cut into 1-1/2 inch cubes

1 tsp cayenne pepper

3 x 14 oz. cans whole tomatoes

1 tsp salt and freshly ground black pepper

2 whole cardamom pods

1 cinnamon stick

4 potatoes, cut into chunks

1/2 tsp garam masala (see recipe below)

GARAM MASALA

1 Tbsp. cumin

2 tsp. coriander

2 tsp. cardamon

1-1/2 tsp. cinnamon

1 tsp. pepper

1/2 tsp. nutmeg

1/2 tsp. cloves

1/2 tsp. cayenne

INSTRUCTIONS

Finely chop the ginger, garlic and green chilies. Grind the coriander seeds to a coarse powder in a coffee or spice grinder and set aside.

Heat the oil in a large, heavy saucepan over medium-high heat. Add the onions and cook until golden brown, stirring often, about 5 minutes. Stir in the ginger mixture and cook for 2 minutes.

Add the meat and cook for 1-2 additional minutes, then add the turmeric, cayenne pepper and ground coriander, coating the meat well.

Add the tomatoes and seasoning and stir, then cover and cook on medium-high heat for 10 minutes.

Add the cardamom and cinnamon, and cook for a further 10 minutes.

Add the potatoes, stir, cover and reduce heat to low. Simmer for at least one hour or until the meat is tender.

Sprinkle the garam masala over the curry and rest for at least 15 minutes before serving.

Serve with steamed basmati rice, poppadoms (flatbread), mint yogurt and a tomato/chili sauce. Scatter with fresh coriander just before serving.

John McAteer

BLESBOK BOUD MET YOGURT

INGREDIENTS

1-2 lbs. blesbok roast
35 oz plain yogurt
1 cup bacon bits
1 lb. bacon
1 large onion
Apple jam

INSTRUCTIONS

Put Blesbok meat into large plastic bag and pour yogurt over to coat. Leave Blesbok in the yogurt overnight.

Next morning mix bacon bits with apricot jam and spread onto meat.

Wrap meat in bacon strips, cover with sliced onions and then wrap in foil.

Bake in the oven at 350°F for 4 hours.

COMMENTS ABOUT JOHN FROM TOM NELSON...

Most all of us have heard the adage, "been there, done that," but few can truthfully make that statement. When it comes to the world of big game hunting and adventure travel, John McAteer has earned that right. A compelling storyteller, John will captivate you as a reader as he recounts his adventures.

If there is one individual I would want to sit around a campfire with while sharing and listening to stories, it would be John McAteer.

Tom Nelson

DAY EIGHT

Being able to hunt on Safari in Africa was exciting and everyday was a blessing even though buffalo had managed to evade us we forged foward. Instead, we decided to go after some more plains game. First on my list was an Impala, so we pointed our safari truck into the sun and headed to a water hole about 20 miles west. I hoped we'd also see some hippos and other African game animals on the way.

The impala is a medium sized antelope found in eastern and southern Africa. It is the sole member of the genus Aepycerosich Lichtenstein. It was discovered by German zoologist Hinrich Lichtenstein in 1912. The common impala and dark faced impala can reach speeds between 47 and 56 miles per hour. They are grazers and their main foods are grass, herbs, shrubs and small bushes. The fast running impala only predators are lions, leopards, cheetahs.

As we drove toward our destination, the truck suddenly came to a slow stop. About 260 yards to the left side of the vehicle was a small herd of antelope. The hunting instinct in me was heightened and I had to go on another stalk to check them out. I was excited by the sight, and thankfully my PH had his head on straight and immediately handed me my rifle.

The stalk was in now in full swing. The plains were as flat as a tabletop, which meant we had no cover. So, we started crawling to close the distance. The best we could do was narrow the distance to about 180 yards.

I was using a 7mm mag and was confident this was the right choice. I took a rest on my backpack before centering my crosshairs on the biggest impala. I squeezed the trigger, and the Impala was down. I'd made yet another deposit in my memory bank.

The Dark Continent

IMPALA CASSEROLE

INGREDIENTS

- 2 Tbsp. olive oil
- 2-1/4 lb. impala meat cut into bite-sized pieces
- 1 medium potato, peeled and cubed
- 1 medium onion, chopped
- 2 medium parsnips, peeled and cubed
- 2 medium turnips, peeled and cubed
- 1/2 cup carrots, peeled and sliced
- 1/2 cup leeks, sliced
- 2-1/2 Tbsp. garlic, crushed
- 1 bay leaf
- 1/2 cups red wine
- 1 can whole peeled tomatoes
- 2 Cups prepared beef stock
- 1/8 tsp ground cumin

INSTRUCTIONS

1. Heat the oil in a large saucepan over a high heat. Once it is hot, add the meat and sauté until completely seared. Add the vegetables, garlic and bay leaf, and cook, stirring often, until browned.

2. Add the wine, reduce the heat and allow to simmer without the lid on until the wine has reduced. Add the tomatoes and then enough beef stock to cover the meat. Cover the saucepan and simmer for about 50 minutes until the meat is tender.

3. Add the cumin and season to taste with salt and pepper.

Serve hot with creamy mashed potatoes.

SOUTH AFRICAN IMPALA CAMPFIRE POTJIE POT

INGREDIENTS

- 3-1/2 Tbsp. sunflower oil
- 1/4 lb. bacon, cut into cubes (optional)
- 1 medium) onion, peeled and roughly diced
- 2-4 lbs. boneless impala meat, cut into cubes
- 2 medium carrot (about 1/3 cup), peeled and roughly diced
- 2 tsp sugar
- 1/2 lb. whole baby potatoes
- 1/2 lb. corn on the cobs, sliced into small chunks
- 1 tsp dried sweet oregano
- 2 fresh/dried bay leaves
- 1 tsp salt
- 1/2 tsp freshly ground black pepper
- 1/2 lb. dried apricots
- 1/2 cup good-quality South African dry red wine
- 4 cups beef/chicken stock

INSTRUCTIONS

Heat half of the sunflower oil in a medium traditional **potjie pot** (cast iron, lidded pot with feet) on a hot fire. Sauté the bacon, if desired, until crispy. Add the onions and continue to sauté until the onions are golden brown Remove the bacon and onions from the pot and set aside.

Add the remaining sunflower oil and brown the impala cubes. Remove from pot and set aside.

Potjie pot

Add the carrots and sugar to the pot and sauté until the sugar has melted and the carrots are caramelized.

Begin layering your potjie pot with the ingredients, starting with the impala cubes, bacon and onion mixture, carrots, baby potatoes, corn chunks, spices, salt and pepper and apricots. Add the red wine and stock and leave to cook for about 4 hours.

Serve with traditional African ipapa (grits), samp (similar to hominy), Mielie Meal (similar to polenta) or rice.

WARTHOG

COMMENTS ABOUT JOHN FROM RUSS THORNBERRY...

"If you're not already a fan of John McAteer's writings you will be when you read his newest book: 'The Dark Continent.' It will entertain you and I guarantee it will compel you to experience the intrigue of African hunting for yourself!

Russ Thornberry

DAY NINE

Today was the day that I was finally going to get to see the famous watering hole I'd heard so much about. Because there aren't any springs in the area, this waterhole was the only source of water for miles around.

This was the day for hunting a nice warthog. A member of the pig family, the warthog has acclimated well to arid heat of the area, but still likes a cool drink of water. They can reach a weight of 130 to 330 pounds and live 7 to 11 years. Their diet consists of grass, roots, berries, and insects. They usually have large litters, and the males use their large tusks to defend themselves.

Since I started talking about going to Africa, I'd been thinking about harvesting a large male warthog. Today I hoped I'd get my chance.

As made our way to our destination, I was amazed by the beauty of the of the planes. Even though it was dry and hot, there was still beauty to be found. Could be my excitement at living out one of my dreams colored my perception a bit.

We approached the waterhole on foot. About 100 yards in front of our destination, we saw some impala, zebra, blue wildebeest, and blesbok. We ended up spooking them as we approached and set up.

We found a good vantage point for watching the waterhole. Not too long after we were settled, we saw a small group of Warthogs working their way to water hole to get a drink.

There were two nice males in the group, and one had a great set of tusks — not the largest, but a nice representation. I decide to take a shot at him, and in an instant, I had my warthog. I was very happy hunter.

The Dark Continent

WARTHOG STEAK WITH CARAMELIZED APPLES

WARTHOG INGREDIENTS
3 Tbsp. tomato sauce
2 Tbsp. soy sauce
2 bay leaves
1 Tbsp. chopped fresh sage
Splash of white wine
1 Tbsp. whole black peppercorns

CARAMELIZED APPLES
2 Tbsp. golden syrup (you can substitute light corn syrup or honey or see recipe on next page)
1 Tbsp. butter

Two 8-oz. warthog or pork fillets
Kosher salt
Butter, for frying
1/4 cup barbecue sauce, for serving

1 Tbsp. brown sugar
2 medium apples, unpeeled, cored and roughly chopped
1/4 cup barbecue sauce, for serving

INSTRUCTIONS

For the warthog: Put the tomato sauce, soy sauce, bay leaves, sage, black peppercorns and white wine in a bowl, add the warthog fillets and marinate at room temperature for 30 minutes.

Meanwhile, make the apples: Heat the golden syrup, butter and sugar together in a small frying pan until melted and starting to caramelize. Add the apples and toss to coat and soften a bit, about 3 minutes. Set aside.

To finish the warthog: Season the warthog fillets with salt. Heat a little butter in a frying pan and fry the warthog until just cooked through, 4 to 5 minutes on each side.

Serve immediately with the caramelized apples and some barbecue sauce.

GOLDEN SYRUP

INGREDIENTS

3 Tbsp. water
1/2 cup [115 g] sugar
1 lemon slice
2 1/2 [500g] cups sugar
1 1/4 cup [310 ml] boiling water

INSTRUCTIONS

Pour 3 Tbsp. water and 1/2 cup sugar into a saucepan, and bring to a simmer over medium-low to medium heat.

While waiting for the mixture to cook, boil 1-1/4 cups water. Once the mixture turns a caramel color, slowly and carefully pour in the boiling water.

Add 2-1/2 cups sugar and bring to a low simmer, then add lemon slice. The lemon will keep the syrup from crystallizing as it simmers.

Turn the heat down to low and let the syrup simmer for about 45 minutes.

Remove the lemon slice and let syrup cool down for a few minutes before pouring it into a sterilized glass jar. The syrup will be thin at this point, but will thicken as it cools.

Store in a cool, dry place.

NOTE: *Nothing else tastes like this golden syrup, so it's worth the effort to make it and use for all sorts of things besides this recipe, including pancakes, waffles, French toast, scones, ice cream, fruit salad, and it can even be used in recipes as a substitute for honey.*

SOUTH AFRICAN WARTHOG BRAAI (BBQ)

The recommended method of cooking warthog according to this game recipe is over the coals of an open fire — better known as a braai in South Africa, or a BBQ in most other parts of the western world.

- 1 large slab of warthog ribs
- 1-1/2 Tbsp. cooking oil (sunflower is good)
- 4 large onions, peeled and sliced
- 1 small chili, seeded and finely chopped (if you like hot, spicy food, leave the seeds in)
- 2 Tbsp. brown sugar
- 2 Tbsp. curry powder (however mild or hot as you like)
- 1 tsp. salt
- 1 tsp. turmeric
- 2 Tbsp. smooth apricot or peach jam
- 2 cups dry white wine

MARINADE INSTRUCTIONS

Heat the cooking oil in a pan on the stove and cook the chopped onion until it is soft and translucent. Add the chili and curry powder and cook gently while stirring. Add the rest of the ingredients, stir, and allow the mixture to simmer gently for about five minutes. Let marinade cool. Put the meat into a large dish or bag and pour the marinade over it. Put in refrigerator and leave overnight.

Your fire is ready if it's a mass of glowing coals with no flames showing. Remove meat from marinade and pat dry. Cook over file on grid or on BBQ grill for 30 minutes, using the marinade to baste. Turn several times and continue basting until meat is cooked through.

COMMENTS ABOUT JOHN FROM NANCY LEE GYSIN...

Being from NY and spending half my life in the construction industry and the other half in the Hunting, Fish & Outdoor industry, it is almost impossible not to know and respect John McAteer as a businessman and conservationist through hunting.

John has the tenacity to excel in what his passions are. There is never a problem, just some bumps in the road that he takes on and respects as a challenge. I respect how seasoned he is from his past efforts with the Long Island SCI Chapter to his worldwide experiences as a dedicated hunter, archer and outdoorsman. John always has the time to introduce and educate new members (young & old) to our hunting community and never makes them feel insecure. They are encouraged by the passion that he portrays and his attention to ethics.

Michael Delfino, Nancy's father, was also a great outdoorsman.

Even though John and I hadn't seen each other for some years, when we were reacquainted, it was like we never skipped a beat. I look forward to seeing more of John, I am honored to call him a friend and counting down the days till we can share camp next to a fire and enjoy the glory that Mother Nature has gifted us.

There is no doubt in my mind that I am a better hunter and conservationist due to John as an archery advocate and a respected voice for the true ethical outdoorsman.

Nancy Lee Gysin
Avula Safaris

DAY TEN

My last day on safari started with a fine breakfast of eggs, warthog sausage, fresh orange juice, and some homemade bread. As I started to put my gear together, I realized I was really going to miss this great continent. Today, I wanted to return to the watering hole in search of a Steenbok (*Raphicerus campestris*). This is another antelope species that only stands 16 to 24 inches. They like dry climates, open plains and grassy vegetation, because they can hide well in tall grass.

Joe Ferraro with a red hartebeest.

We utilized strategy when approaching the waterhole this time, and had prepared ourselves for a long day. As we waited, we saw lots of other animals, including rhinos and some more zebra.

About 2 p.m., we spotted three female steenbok but there were no males with them. So, we watched as they worked their way down to water. They spent the better part of 30 minutes around the area, always on guard and looking for predators.

When they finally walked off, I saw a red hartebeest in the distance but it would not commit to coming any closer. I ranged him at 450 yards. Even though I have taken shots from that distance, something was telling me to wait. I figured he would eventually come in closer so I'd have a better shot.

As I waited, I suddenly lost track of the hartebeest. I looked around to see where he'd gone, and spotted a lioness approaching on the same path the hartebeest had just been traveling.

With that chance blown, we sat and waited some more. Finally, spotted a visitor — a nice male steenbok. I didn't even think before I brought my rifle up and took the shot. All it took to get this trophy was a little patience.

STEENBOK SKEWERS

INGREDIENTS

- Steenbok steaks cut into 1/4-inch cubes
- 4 Tbsp. hoisin sauce
- 1/4 cup soy sauce
- 1 Tbsp. olive oil
- 1 Tbsp. minced fresh ginger root
- 1/4 cup cilantro chopped
- 2 garlic cloves minced
- 1 white onion
- 2-3 Jalapenos (optional)

INSTRUCTIONS

Mix together hoisin sauce, soy sauce, garlic, olive oil, cilantro and ginger.

Cut steenbok steaks into 1/4-inch cubes across grain on a diagonal. Place meat in a 1-gallon resealable plastic bag. Pour hoisin sauce mixture over slices, and mix well. Refrigerate 1 hour or overnight.

Preheat an outdoor grill for high heat. Discard the marinade and thread steenbok pieces onto skewers with onion and jalapeno slices in between each piece.

Grill skewers 3 minutes per side, or to desired doneness.

Serve with a fresh salad and a side of hoisin sauce for extra dipping!

STEENBOK MEATLOAF WITH SPICY KETCHUP

INGREDIENTS

1.5 lbs ground steenbok
1/2 cup panko or plain breadcrumbs
1 egg, beaten
1 Tbsp. yellow mustard
1 Tbsp. Worcestershire sauce
1 Tbsp. A-1 steak sauce

BLOODY MARY KETCHUP

1 cup ketchup
Red pepper flakes to taste

5 green chard leaves chopped (can substitute spinach)
1 yellow or green zucchini shaved into ribbons
1 garlic clove minced
2 Tbsp. butter

2 tablespoons Bloody Mary seasoning (see recipe on following page)

INSTRUCTIONS

Pre-heat oven to 400°F.

Heat skillet over medium heat. Add 2 tablespoons butter, garlic, chard and zucchini. Cook until soft and wilted. Remove from heat.

In a large bowl combine ground steenbok, panko, egg, mustard, Worcestershire sauce and A-1 and mix well. Add chard and zucchini and stir together.

Form meat into a loaf and place in a baking dish. Cover with foil and bake for 30 minutes.

Remove foil. Spoon Bloody Mary Ketchup on top of meatloaf and continue to cook for 10 minutes or until ketchup has slightly caramelized.

Serve with a side of smashed potatoes.

HOMEMADE BLOODY MARY SEASONING

INGREDIENTS

6 Tbps. grated horseradish

2 Tbsp. Worcestershire sauce

6 big dashes of Tabasco®

1 tsp salt

1 tsp celery salt

1/2 teaspoon celery seed

1 ounce fresh lemon juice

1 ounce olive brine (just the liquid from whatever green olive jar you have on hand)

1 full teaspoon of coarse-ground black pepper.

INSTRUCTIONS

Mix together and refrigerate in an air-tight container.

COMMENTS ABOUT JOHN FROM JIM BOWMAN...

Many men dream of taking to the woods and fields in far off romantic destinations to fulfill our primal need to hunt. We were born predators and dream of being adventurers. The demands of everyday life precludes most of us from ever fulfilling those dreams. But every once in a while there comes along someone who will not be denied. They spend their lives in pursuit of adventure and species only dreamed of by the rest of us. Who has not read or watched the adventures of Fred Bear or Peter Capstic and imagined they were right there with them at their moments of success?

John McAteer is one of those fortunate souls and shares many of his African adventures in the pages of this book.

So settle in and prepare as together we accompany my friend John to the dark continent.

Jim Bowman
Hunter and Singer/Songwriter

DAY ELEVEN

It was a long night and telling a lot of great stories on previous hunts that we were all on, I returned to my rondavel to get a good night sleep. As I drifted off to sleep, I had visions of the next day, knowing that it was going to be my last in Africa. It didn't take long before I fell fast asleep.

When I open my eyes the next morning, I was up and watching a snake slithering in and out of the bindings of the thatched roof. I assumed that the snake had probably lived there its entire life. One thing about hunting in Africa you never know what to expect each morning.

My clothes were neatly folded from the previous day, put on my pants and prepared for a new, exciting day. First on the agenda was one of the most spectacular breakfasts that I had ever eaten. Every meal had been unusual here, and I looked forward to them with great anticipation.

You know the last few days were always exciting because you never knew how the things would unfold and what type of excitement and adventure was just around the corner. Today was like every other day — we loaded our gear into our trucks, preparing another long day. The weather was great; the sun was shining and the temperature was about 45°. I expected it to turn into a warm day because the sun was already shining bright.

The plan today was to travel approximately 40 miles to a new concession area that was known for having exceptional plains game. We entered our new area with high expectations, and were quickly rewarded. The first of many plains game we encountered were water bucks. Since they were mostly immature and not quite what I was looking for, we proceeded down a long red clay road.

Along the way, we stumbled on a few white rhinos and a beautiful giraffe. I was surprised by the amount of real estate they could consume at a full gallop.

My tracker's eyes never left the red clay dirt as he studied every track that we came across. It was mid afternoon

The Dark Continent

when my PH decided we would stop and have a field lunch. Today's lunch included a beautiful salad and warthog spareribs cooked on an open fire with some roasted potatoes. The best part was a nice cold beer, since the temperature had climbed to 80° by this time.

After a great lunch we were back in the truck and in search of some plains game. It wasn't too long before we came across a mature red Lechwe. The Lechwe is in the antelope family and can be found throughout south-central Africa. There are three subspecies of lechwe that are found in South Africa, Botswana and Namibia. The lechwe is what I would consider a medium-sized antelope. The males, called rams, can have a mass of approximately 80 kg. Their hindquarters are noticeably higher than their front, and their horns remind me of a water buck.

Rams are territorial and they usually actively defend their areas. As we approached this beautiful Lechwe, I took out my rangefinder and I ranged it at about 450 yards.

One of the most difficult things to do while hunting in Africa is to find concealment. In this case, we had no cover.

I grabbed my weapon of choice, a 7mm mag made by Browning, and we disembarked from the truck with what we thought was a good game plan.

After trying to close the distance by about 100 yards, the wind shifted, alerting the animals, and our quarry disappeared. We pursued the animal for almost three hours, playing the wind and trying to find cover.

We finally had our quarry in sight again, but he was almost 400 yards from where we were glassing him. We were in an elevated position, so we quickly made a plan.

We started stalking him, using whatever cover we could find. As we maneuvered towards a large anthill, my tracker pointed to the ground about 25 yards in front of us and told us to stop. There in front of us was what I am guessing was a Python. It was the biggest snake I had ever seen in my entire hunting career!

We skirted around him and proceeded to close the distance to 300 yards, and the wind was perfect. The red lechwe was coming toward an opening, which would be the only shot I'd be able to take. I moved over against a thorn bush and came to a good solid rest.

I sat there, waiting for animal to enter the open area, and it seemed to take forever. Finally, about 25 or 30 minutes later, he presented an excellent shot and I took it. At first, I didn't think I'd hit him because as soon as I made the shot, he disappeared.

This was were our excellent tracker earned his pay. While he was looking for my red Lechwe, our tracker made a profound statement I'll never forget, "The dirt never lies." The tracker picked up the trail in the red clay and within hundred yards found my red lechwe.

Africa is one of the most majestic continents I've had the privilege the hunt. Now that my Safari had drawn to an end like all my adventures, I come away with new memories, I cannot wait for the opportunity to go back. The dark continent was a mystic adventure I would recommend to any sportsman or sportswoman . You will not be disappointed!

RED LECHWE TENDERLOIN WITH ROSEMARY BALSAMIC REDUCTION

3 tablespoons of virgin oil
2 tablespoons of finely chopped parsley leaves
2 garlic cloves finely chopped
1 tablespoon of finely chopped rosemary leaves

Mix ingredients in a small bowl, adding salt and pepper to taste. Bring meat to room temperature and cover with mixture. Let the meat sit at room on the counter for 30 minutes.

Preheat your oven to 350°F
Place cast iron skillet over high heat, add 2 tablespoons olive oil and sear meat on each side for 3 minutes or until browned. Remove meat to dish and place in oven for five minutes while you prepare the reduction.

REDUCTION SAUCE

1 tablespoon of olive oil
2 tablespoons of chopped shallots
1 cup balsamic vinegar
1 tablespoon of chopped garlic
1 sprig rosemary, large
2 Tbsp butter

Using the same skillet without cleaning, add olive oil and shallots and cook until translucent, about one minute then add garlic and cook until tender. Add balsamic vinegar, and 1 large Rosemary sprig and bring to boil. Reduce the vinegar until only 1/4 cup remains. Remove from heat and add 2 tablespoons of butter. Stir until melted.

Drizzle sauce over tenderloin and serve.

RED LECHWE, SAGE AND GARLIC SAUSAGE

1 lbs bacon
1-2 lbs ground Lechwe
2 tbsp diced garlic
1 tbsp salt
½ tsp ground black pepper

1/2 tsp mustard powder
1 tsp minced fresh sage
3-4 ft pork sausage casing, washed out
4 pieces of bread

INSTRUCTIONS:
Grind the bacon using the medium sized grinder plate, then mix all of the ingredients, except the bread and casing, together. When mixed, grind using medium-sized grinder plate. Place mixture in the freezer for 15-20 minutes.

Install sausage tube on the meat grinder, then thread casing onto the sausage tube. Add mixture to grinder and push until it appears at the end of the tube. Pull a portion of the casing past the tube opening and knot the casing. Pull back the casing snug to the tube

Use one hand to allow the casing to slowly slide off of the tube as you feed the mixture with the other hand. You want to prevent air bubbles from forming. Feed the mixture into the casing until all meat is gone.

Feed chunks of bread into the casing until the meat has filled the casing. Remove the casing from the tube, and squeeze bread from casing. Knot casing snuggly against meat. Cut the casing near the knot.

Bring your grill to medium high heat and cook for 15-20 minutes, flipping occasionally.

SOMETHING TO CHEW ON

Here is some food for thought. Most hunters that travel to South Africa are great conservationists. Almost all of the meat that is harvested during these traditional hunts is donated. If you've ever been on an African safari, you know that some of this meat will be eaten by the hunters, but most of it is given to the local poor and rural areas and communities.

This meat is a crucial addition to the otherwise low-protein diets of much of the population. I don't think there are any numbers quantifying how much of the game meat goes to local communities, but one thing is for sure — it's the difference between life and death in some cases for these impoverished people. Many communities benefit from this, but hardly anything is ever said about this effort.

It is easy to mock a hunter who enjoys the sport and make them out as some kind of mercenary. This is a wake-up call to all sportsmen — fight for what you believe in, teach our young the beauty of enjoying the outdoors and let them see what you have learned by teaching them everything you know.

The hunting industry, as we all know, is failing because due to bad public relations. We need to educate people and show them that just because we are hunters, we don't just throw away what we harvest — we share it with those in need.

One of our industries great legends **Bob Foulkrod** giving back to native villages the bounty of his hunting adventure by suppling fresh meat to people. Bob is a true conservationist and one of the most ethical hunters that I have ever had the privilege of calling my good friend.

The Dark Continent

I am proud of **Bob Foulkrod** and **SAPA** for all the hard work they do. There recognition and ability to share and give back is something that needs to be brought to lite currently.

Villagers travel a great distance to receive this generous food donated by hunters

One of the open markets where villagers sell handmade items.

My first South African currency.

FRIENDS AND FELLOW HUNTERS

John McAteer, Joseph Ferraro, and Michael Delfino.

Joseph Ferraro with a warthog he harvested.

Mark Drury with a turkey he harvested.

Michael Delfino with a male lion he harvested.

Bob Foulkrod with a bull elephant he harvested.

CLOSING STATEMENT

As my African adventure concluded, I was already looking forward to coming back to this great continent. I would truly recommend to all my fellow sportsmen to hunt the dark continent if offered the opportunity. There is a tremendous amount of excitement involved in an African safari.

I would like to leave you with a bit of inspiration. Every day must come to an end, but the beauty of that statement is that tomorrow brings a new day, and with it comes another new adventure. Always feed your ambition, because without it, there is no future.

As sportsmen we need to protect the great outdoors, and we must do everything ethically and with conservation in mind so that future generations can enjoy what we have enjoyed. Always try to pass on what you have learned in life to the younger generations and hope they in turn will pass it on as they mature.

I hope you have enjoyed the book it comes from a common man on a common quest, the love of the outdoors.

Hunt hard, and hunt safe,

John McAteer

John McAteer

ALSO AVAILABLE FROM JOHN McATEER

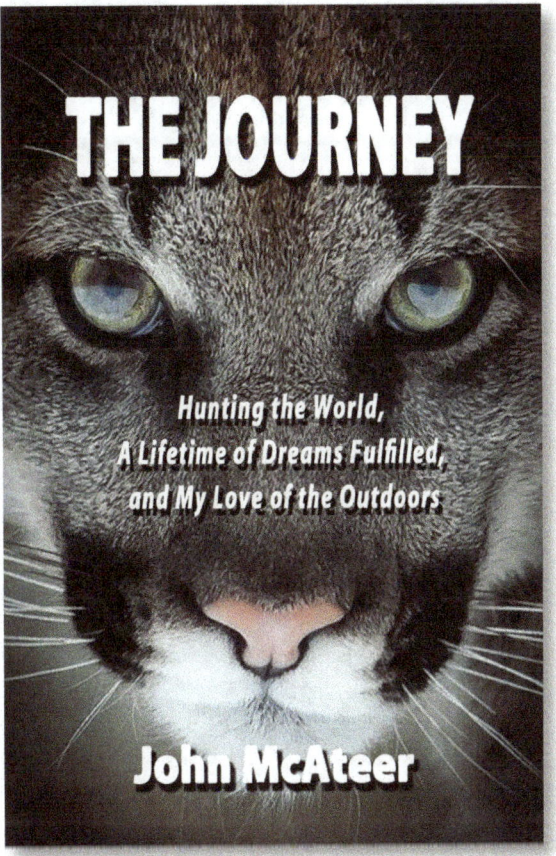

Life is a journey with many twists and turns. For John McAteer, they came in the form of mountains, rivers and streams. He has experienced many rewarding and truly fascinating moments in the great outdoors, and feels blessed to be able to work outside and deal with the natural world. In this book, John shares his experiences of hunting all over the world, the interesting people he met while doing this and some tasty recipes for the amazing animals he harvested.

AVAILABLE IN HARDCOVER, PAPERBACK & EBOOK FORMATS
@ AMAZON, BARNES & NOBLE
AND OTHER ONLINE RETAILERS

www.ingramcontent.com/pod-product-compliance
Lightning Source LLC
Chambersburg PA
CBHW062113280426
43661CB00086B/613